50 Low Sodium Comfort Food for a Healthier Heart

By: Kelly Johnson

Table of Contents

- Baked Macaroni and Cheese with Cauliflower
- Grilled Chicken and Vegetable Skewers
- Sweet Potato Shepherd's Pie
- Veggie-Stuffed Bell Peppers
- Zucchini Noodles with Pesto
- Roasted Turkey with Garlic and Herbs
- Lentil Soup with Carrots and Celery
- Quinoa Stuffed Mushrooms
- Baked Chicken Parmesan with Whole Wheat Breadcrumbs
- Cauliflower Mashed Potatoes
- Chickpea and Spinach Stew
- Turkey Meatballs in Tomato Sauce
- Roasted Salmon with Lemon and Dill
- Sweet and Sour Chicken with Brown Rice
- Baked Sweet Potatoes with Black Beans
- Grilled Veggie Tacos with Avocado
- Spaghetti Squash with Marinara Sauce
- Cauliflower Fried Rice
- Homemade Veggie Burgers
- Chicken and Vegetable Stir-Fry
- Baked Falafel with Cucumber Yogurt Sauce
- Whole Wheat Pancakes with Fresh Fruit
- Eggplant Parmesan with Low-Sodium Marinara
- Baked Lemon Herb Salmon
- Stuffed Acorn Squash with Quinoa
- Roasted Root Vegetables with Olive Oil
- Chicken and Brown Rice Casserole
- Black Bean and Sweet Potato Chili
- Zucchini Fritters with Greek Yogurt Dip
- Lentil Tacos with Guacamole
- Grilled Portobello Mushrooms with Balsamic Glaze
- Broccoli and Cheddar Quiche
- Spaghetti with Roasted Tomato Sauce
- Grilled Shrimp with Cilantro-Lime Rice
- Baked Turkey Breast with Rosemary

- Veggie-Packed Minestrone Soup
- Grilled Veggie and Hummus Wraps
- Roasted Butternut Squash with Garlic and Sage
- Black Bean and Quinoa Salad
- Lemon Garlic Roasted Chicken
- Baked Sweet Potato Fries
- Grilled Tofu Stir-Fry with Veggies
- Low-Sodium Beef Stew with Vegetables
- Vegan Lentil Loaf
- Roasted Chickpeas for Snacking
- Baked Chicken Tenders with Almond Flour
- Spaghetti Squash with Garlic and Olive Oil
- Avocado and Tomato Salad with Balsamic Dressing
- Baked Veggie Quesadillas
- Sweet Potato and Kale Salad

Baked Macaroni and Cheese with Cauliflower

Ingredients

- 8 oz elbow macaroni
- 2 cups cauliflower florets
- 2 tbsp butter
- 2 tbsp all-purpose flour
- 2 cups unsweetened almond milk
- 2 cups shredded vegan cheese
- 1/2 cup breadcrumbs
- 1/4 tsp garlic powder
- 1/4 tsp onion powder
- Salt and pepper, to taste

Instructions

1. Preheat the oven to 375°F (190°C).
2. Cook the macaroni according to package directions. Drain and set aside.
3. Steam the cauliflower florets until tender, about 7-10 minutes.
4. In a large saucepan, melt the butter over medium heat. Add the flour and whisk constantly for 1-2 minutes.
5. Gradually add the almond milk while whisking to avoid lumps. Continue cooking and stirring until the sauce thickens.
6. Stir in the vegan cheese, garlic powder, onion powder, salt, and pepper. Mix until the cheese is melted and smooth.
7. Add the cooked macaroni and cauliflower to the cheese sauce and stir to combine.
8. Pour the mixture into a greased baking dish, top with breadcrumbs, and bake for 15-20 minutes, until golden and bubbly.

Grilled Chicken and Vegetable Skewers

Ingredients

- 2 boneless, skinless chicken breasts, cut into chunks
- 1 red bell pepper, cut into chunks
- 1 zucchini, sliced
- 1 red onion, cut into chunks
- 1/2 cup olive oil
- 2 tbsp lemon juice
- 2 tbsp fresh parsley, chopped
- 1 tsp garlic powder
- Salt and pepper, to taste

Instructions

1. Preheat the grill to medium-high heat.
2. In a bowl, whisk together olive oil, lemon juice, parsley, garlic powder, salt, and pepper.
3. Thread the chicken and vegetables onto skewers, alternating between the chicken and the vegetables.
4. Brush the skewers with the marinade mixture.
5. Grill the skewers for 10-12 minutes, turning occasionally, until the chicken is cooked through and the vegetables are tender.
6. Serve the skewers with a side of rice or a fresh salad.

Sweet Potato Shepherd's Pie

Ingredients

- 4 large sweet potatoes, peeled and cubed
- 1 tbsp olive oil
- 1/2 cup diced onion
- 2 garlic cloves, minced
- 1 cup lentils, cooked
- 1 cup carrots, diced
- 1 cup peas
- 2 tbsp tomato paste
- 1 tsp dried thyme
- 1 tsp dried rosemary
- 1/4 cup vegetable broth
- Salt and pepper, to taste

Instructions

1. Preheat the oven to 375°F (190°C).
2. Boil the sweet potatoes in salted water for about 10-12 minutes until tender. Drain and mash with a little olive oil and salt. Set aside.
3. In a large skillet, heat olive oil over medium heat. Add the onion and garlic, and sauté until softened.
4. Add the cooked lentils, carrots, peas, tomato paste, thyme, rosemary, and vegetable broth to the skillet. Cook for 5-7 minutes, until heated through and tender.
5. Season with salt and pepper.
6. Transfer the lentil mixture to a baking dish, and top with the mashed sweet potatoes.
7. Bake for 20-25 minutes, until the top is lightly golden.

Veggie-Stuffed Bell Peppers

Ingredients

- 4 bell peppers, tops cut off and seeds removed
- 1 cup cooked quinoa
- 1/2 cup black beans, drained and rinsed
- 1/2 cup corn kernels
- 1/4 cup diced tomatoes
- 1 tsp cumin
- 1 tsp chili powder
- 1/2 tsp garlic powder
- 1/2 tsp salt
- 1/4 tsp black pepper
- 1/4 cup vegan cheese (optional)

Instructions

1. Preheat the oven to 375°F (190°C).
2. In a large bowl, combine the quinoa, black beans, corn, diced tomatoes, cumin, chili powder, garlic powder, salt, and pepper.
3. Stuff the bell peppers with the quinoa mixture.
4. Place the stuffed peppers in a baking dish and cover with aluminum foil.
5. Bake for 30-35 minutes, until the peppers are tender.
6. If using, sprinkle the tops with vegan cheese and bake for an additional 5 minutes until the cheese melts.

Zucchini Noodles with Pesto

Ingredients

- 2 medium zucchinis, spiralized into noodles
- 1 cup fresh basil leaves
- 1/4 cup pine nuts
- 1/4 cup nutritional yeast
- 2 garlic cloves
- 1/4 cup olive oil
- Salt and pepper, to taste

Instructions

1. In a food processor, combine the basil, pine nuts, nutritional yeast, garlic, olive oil, salt, and pepper. Pulse until smooth.
2. In a large skillet, heat a little olive oil over medium heat. Add the zucchini noodles and cook for 2-3 minutes, until tender but still al dente.
3. Toss the noodles with the pesto and serve immediately.

Roasted Turkey with Garlic and Herbs

Ingredients

- 1 whole turkey (10-12 lbs)
- 1/4 cup olive oil
- 4 garlic cloves, minced
- 2 tbsp fresh thyme, chopped
- 2 tbsp fresh rosemary, chopped
- 1 tbsp lemon juice
- Salt and pepper, to taste

Instructions

1. Preheat the oven to 325°F (165°C).
2. In a small bowl, combine olive oil, garlic, thyme, rosemary, lemon juice, salt, and pepper.
3. Rub the turkey with the olive oil mixture, making sure to cover the skin evenly.
4. Roast the turkey in the oven for 2.5-3 hours, or until the internal temperature reaches 165°F (75°C).
5. Let the turkey rest for 20 minutes before carving.

Lentil Soup with Carrots and Celery

Ingredients

- 1 cup dried lentils, rinsed
- 1 onion, diced
- 2 carrots, peeled and chopped
- 2 celery stalks, chopped
- 2 garlic cloves, minced
- 1 tsp cumin
- 1 tsp turmeric
- 1 bay leaf
- 4 cups vegetable broth
- Salt and pepper, to taste

Instructions

1. In a large pot, sauté the onion, carrots, celery, and garlic in olive oil over medium heat for 5-7 minutes, until softened.
2. Add the cumin, turmeric, and bay leaf, and cook for 1 minute.
3. Stir in the lentils and vegetable broth. Bring to a boil, then reduce heat and simmer for 30-40 minutes, until the lentils are tender.
4. Season with salt and pepper, and remove the bay leaf before serving.

Quinoa Stuffed Mushrooms

Ingredients

- 12 large mushroom caps, stems removed
- 1 cup cooked quinoa
- 1/4 cup sun-dried tomatoes, chopped
- 1/4 cup fresh spinach, chopped
- 2 tbsp nutritional yeast
- 1/4 tsp garlic powder
- Salt and pepper, to taste
- 2 tbsp olive oil

Instructions

1. Preheat the oven to 375°F (190°C).
2. In a bowl, combine the cooked quinoa, sun-dried tomatoes, spinach, nutritional yeast, garlic powder, salt, and pepper.
3. Stuff the mushroom caps with the quinoa mixture and place them on a baking sheet.
4. Drizzle with olive oil and bake for 20-25 minutes, until the mushrooms are tender.
5. Serve warm as an appetizer or side dish.

Baked Chicken Parmesan with Whole Wheat Breadcrumbs

Ingredients

- 4 boneless, skinless chicken breasts
- 1 cup whole wheat breadcrumbs
- 1/2 cup grated Parmesan cheese
- 1/2 cup marinara sauce
- 1 1/2 cups shredded mozzarella cheese
- 1 egg, beaten
- 1 tbsp olive oil
- Salt and pepper, to taste

Instructions

1. Preheat the oven to 375°F (190°C).
2. Season the chicken breasts with salt and pepper.
3. In a shallow bowl, combine the whole wheat breadcrumbs and Parmesan cheese.
4. Dip each chicken breast in the beaten egg, then coat with the breadcrumb mixture.
5. Heat olive oil in a skillet over medium heat. Brown each side of the chicken breasts for 2-3 minutes.
6. Transfer the chicken to a baking dish. Spoon marinara sauce over each chicken breast and sprinkle with mozzarella cheese.
7. Bake for 20-25 minutes, until the chicken is cooked through and the cheese is melted and bubbly.

Cauliflower Mashed Potatoes

Ingredients

- 1 head of cauliflower, chopped into florets
- 2 tbsp olive oil or butter
- 1/4 cup unsweetened almond milk
- 2 garlic cloves, minced
- Salt and pepper, to taste

Instructions

1. Steam or boil the cauliflower florets for about 10 minutes until tender.
2. In a skillet, heat the olive oil or butter over medium heat and sauté the garlic until fragrant, about 1-2 minutes.
3. Drain the cauliflower and transfer to a food processor. Add the sautéed garlic, almond milk, salt, and pepper.
4. Blend until smooth and creamy. Adjust the texture by adding more almond milk if needed.
5. Serve as a low-carb alternative to mashed potatoes.

Chickpea and Spinach Stew

Ingredients

- 2 cups cooked chickpeas (or 1 can, drained and rinsed)
- 4 cups fresh spinach
- 1 onion, diced
- 2 garlic cloves, minced
- 1 can diced tomatoes
- 1 tsp ground cumin
- 1 tsp turmeric
- 1 tsp paprika
- 1/2 tsp chili powder
- 2 cups vegetable broth
- Salt and pepper, to taste

Instructions

1. In a large pot, sauté the onion and garlic over medium heat until softened.
2. Add the cumin, turmeric, paprika, and chili powder, and cook for 1 minute.
3. Stir in the chickpeas, diced tomatoes, vegetable broth, salt, and pepper.
4. Bring to a boil, then reduce heat and simmer for 15-20 minutes.
5. Add the spinach and cook until wilted.
6. Serve the stew with a slice of whole-grain bread or over rice.

Turkey Meatballs in Tomato Sauce

Ingredients

- 1 lb ground turkey
- 1/4 cup breadcrumbs
- 1 egg
- 1/4 cup grated Parmesan cheese
- 2 tbsp fresh parsley, chopped
- 1/2 tsp garlic powder
- 1/4 tsp onion powder
- 1 jar marinara sauce
- Salt and pepper, to taste

Instructions

1. Preheat the oven to 375°F (190°C).
2. In a large bowl, combine the ground turkey, breadcrumbs, egg, Parmesan cheese, parsley, garlic powder, onion powder, salt, and pepper.
3. Roll the mixture into small meatballs and place on a greased baking sheet.
4. Bake for 20-25 minutes, until the meatballs are cooked through.
5. In a large saucepan, heat the marinara sauce over medium heat. Add the meatballs to the sauce and simmer for 10 minutes.
6. Serve the meatballs over spaghetti or with a side of steamed vegetables.

Roasted Salmon with Lemon and Dill

Ingredients

- 4 salmon fillets
- 2 tbsp olive oil
- 1 lemon, sliced
- 2 tbsp fresh dill, chopped
- Salt and pepper, to taste

Instructions

1. Preheat the oven to 400°F (200°C).
2. Place the salmon fillets on a baking sheet lined with parchment paper.
3. Drizzle with olive oil and season with salt and pepper.
4. Top with lemon slices and sprinkle with fresh dill.
5. Roast for 12-15 minutes, or until the salmon is cooked through and flakes easily with a fork.
6. Serve with a side of roasted vegetables or quinoa.

Sweet and Sour Chicken with Brown Rice

Ingredients

- 1 lb boneless, skinless chicken breasts, cut into chunks
- 1 tbsp olive oil
- 1 onion, sliced
- 1 bell pepper, sliced
- 1/2 cup pineapple chunks
- 1/4 cup apple cider vinegar
- 1/4 cup honey
- 1/4 cup soy sauce
- 2 tbsp ketchup
- 2 cups cooked brown rice

Instructions

1. Heat olive oil in a skillet over medium heat. Add the chicken chunks and cook until browned on all sides, about 8-10 minutes.
2. Remove the chicken from the skillet and set aside.
3. In the same skillet, sauté the onion and bell pepper until softened, about 5 minutes.
4. Add the pineapple, apple cider vinegar, honey, soy sauce, and ketchup to the skillet. Stir to combine.
5. Return the chicken to the skillet and cook for an additional 5-7 minutes, until the sauce has thickened.
6. Serve the sweet and sour chicken over the cooked brown rice.

Baked Sweet Potatoes with Black Beans

Ingredients

- 4 medium sweet potatoes
- 1 can black beans, drained and rinsed
- 1 tsp cumin
- 1/2 tsp chili powder
- 1/2 tsp garlic powder
- 1/4 cup cilantro, chopped
- 1/4 cup salsa (optional)
- Salt and pepper, to taste

Instructions

1. Preheat the oven to 400°F (200°C).
2. Pierce the sweet potatoes with a fork and place them on a baking sheet.
3. Bake for 40-45 minutes, or until the sweet potatoes are soft and cooked through.
4. While the sweet potatoes bake, heat the black beans in a saucepan over medium heat. Add the cumin, chili powder, garlic powder, salt, and pepper. Stir to combine and cook for 5-7 minutes.
5. Once the sweet potatoes are done, cut them open and fluff with a fork.
6. Top with the spiced black beans, cilantro, and a spoonful of salsa, if desired.

Grilled Veggie Tacos with Avocado

Ingredients

- 2 zucchinis, sliced
- 1 red bell pepper, sliced
- 1 yellow bell pepper, sliced
- 1 red onion, sliced
- 1 tbsp olive oil
- 1 tsp cumin
- 1 tsp chili powder
- Salt and pepper, to taste
- 8 small corn tortillas
- 1 avocado, sliced
- Fresh cilantro, for garnish
- Lime wedges, for serving

Instructions

1. Preheat a grill or grill pan over medium heat.
2. Toss the zucchini, bell peppers, and onion with olive oil, cumin, chili powder, salt, and pepper.
3. Grill the veggies for 5-7 minutes on each side, until tender and slightly charred.
4. Warm the tortillas on the grill for about 1 minute.
5. To assemble, place the grilled veggies on each tortilla, top with avocado slices, and garnish with fresh cilantro and a squeeze of lime juice.
6. Serve with additional lime wedges on the side.

Spaghetti Squash with Marinara Sauce

Ingredients

- 1 medium spaghetti squash
- 2 cups marinara sauce
- 1 tbsp olive oil
- Salt and pepper, to taste
- Fresh basil, for garnish
- Grated Parmesan cheese (optional)

Instructions

1. Preheat the oven to 400°F (200°C).
2. Cut the spaghetti squash in half lengthwise and remove the seeds.
3. Drizzle with olive oil, and season with salt and pepper. Place the squash halves cut-side down on a baking sheet.
4. Roast for 30-40 minutes, until the squash is tender and can be shredded with a fork.
5. While the squash is roasting, heat the marinara sauce in a saucepan over medium heat.
6. Once the squash is cooked, use a fork to scrape the flesh into spaghetti-like strands.
7. Top with marinara sauce, fresh basil, and grated Parmesan cheese, if desired.

Cauliflower Fried Rice

Ingredients

- 1 small head of cauliflower, grated into rice-sized pieces
- 1 tbsp sesame oil
- 2 eggs, lightly beaten
- 1/2 cup peas and carrots (frozen or fresh)
- 2 green onions, chopped
- 2 tbsp soy sauce
- 1 tbsp rice vinegar
- 1 garlic clove, minced
- Salt and pepper, to taste

Instructions

1. Heat sesame oil in a large skillet or wok over medium heat.
2. Add the garlic and cook for 1 minute, until fragrant.
3. Add the peas and carrots, and cook for 2-3 minutes until tender.
4. Push the vegetables to one side of the skillet and pour the beaten eggs into the other side. Scramble the eggs until cooked.
5. Add the grated cauliflower rice and cook for 5-7 minutes, stirring frequently, until tender.
6. Stir in the soy sauce, rice vinegar, and green onions. Season with salt and pepper to taste.
7. Serve hot as a healthy, low-carb alternative to regular fried rice.

Homemade Veggie Burgers

Ingredients

- 1 can (15 oz) black beans, drained and mashed
- 1/2 cup cooked quinoa
- 1/4 cup breadcrumbs
- 1/4 cup grated carrot
- 1/4 cup chopped spinach
- 1 tbsp soy sauce
- 1 tsp garlic powder
- 1/2 tsp cumin
- 1/4 tsp smoked paprika
- Salt and pepper, to taste
- 1 tbsp olive oil

Instructions

1. In a bowl, combine the mashed black beans, cooked quinoa, breadcrumbs, grated carrot, spinach, soy sauce, garlic powder, cumin, paprika, salt, and pepper.
2. Shape the mixture into 4 burger patties.
3. Heat olive oil in a skillet over medium heat.
4. Cook the patties for 4-5 minutes per side, until golden and crispy.
5. Serve the veggie burgers on whole-grain buns with your favorite toppings, such as avocado, lettuce, and tomato.

Chicken and Vegetable Stir-Fry

Ingredients

- 2 chicken breasts, sliced into thin strips
- 1 tbsp olive oil
- 1 red bell pepper, sliced
- 1 yellow bell pepper, sliced
- 1 cup broccoli florets
- 1 carrot, julienned
- 2 garlic cloves, minced
- 2 tbsp soy sauce
- 1 tbsp rice vinegar
- 1 tsp honey
- Salt and pepper, to taste

Instructions

1. Heat olive oil in a large skillet or wok over medium-high heat.
2. Add the chicken strips and cook for 5-7 minutes, until browned and cooked through. Remove the chicken and set aside.
3. In the same skillet, add the garlic and vegetables. Stir-fry for 3-4 minutes, until tender.
4. In a small bowl, mix the soy sauce, rice vinegar, and honey.
5. Return the chicken to the skillet, pour the sauce over the chicken and veggies, and stir to coat.
6. Cook for an additional 2-3 minutes. Season with salt and pepper to taste.
7. Serve hot over brown rice or noodles.

Baked Falafel with Cucumber Yogurt Sauce

Ingredients for Falafel

- 1 can (15 oz) chickpeas, drained and rinsed
- 1/4 cup chopped parsley
- 1/4 cup chopped cilantro
- 1/4 cup onion, chopped
- 2 garlic cloves, minced
- 1 tsp cumin
- 1/2 tsp coriander
- 1 tbsp olive oil
- 1/4 cup flour (or chickpea flour)
- Salt and pepper, to taste

Ingredients for Cucumber Yogurt Sauce

- 1/2 cup plain Greek yogurt
- 1/4 cup cucumber, finely chopped
- 1 tbsp lemon juice
- 1 tbsp fresh dill, chopped
- Salt and pepper, to taste

Instructions

1. Preheat the oven to 375°F (190°C).
2. In a food processor, combine chickpeas, parsley, cilantro, onion, garlic, cumin, coriander, olive oil, flour, salt, and pepper. Pulse until smooth.
3. Shape the mixture into small balls or patties and place on a baking sheet lined with parchment paper.
4. Bake for 20-25 minutes, flipping halfway through, until golden and crisp.
5. For the sauce, mix the yogurt, cucumber, lemon juice, dill, salt, and pepper in a bowl.
6. Serve the falafel with the cucumber yogurt sauce.

Whole Wheat Pancakes with Fresh Fruit

Ingredients

- 1 1/2 cups whole wheat flour
- 1 tbsp baking powder
- 1/2 tsp salt
- 1 cup almond milk
- 1 egg
- 2 tbsp maple syrup
- 1 tsp vanilla extract
- 1 tbsp olive oil
- Fresh fruit (strawberries, blueberries, bananas), for topping

Instructions

1. In a large bowl, whisk together the whole wheat flour, baking powder, and salt.
2. In a separate bowl, whisk the almond milk, egg, maple syrup, and vanilla extract.
3. Pour the wet ingredients into the dry ingredients and stir until just combined.
4. Heat a non-stick skillet or griddle over medium heat and lightly grease with olive oil.
5. Pour batter onto the skillet, cooking each pancake for 2-3 minutes on each side, until golden brown.
6. Serve the pancakes with fresh fruit and a drizzle of maple syrup.

Eggplant Parmesan with Low-Sodium Marinara

Ingredients

- 2 medium eggplants, sliced into 1/2-inch rounds
- 1 cup whole wheat breadcrumbs
- 1/2 cup grated Parmesan cheese
- 2 eggs, beaten
- 1 jar low-sodium marinara sauce
- 1 1/2 cups shredded mozzarella cheese
- Fresh basil, for garnish

Instructions

1. Preheat the oven to 375°F (190°C).
2. Dip each eggplant slice in the beaten eggs, then coat with breadcrumbs and Parmesan cheese.
3. Place the breaded eggplant slices on a baking sheet lined with parchment paper. Bake for 20-25 minutes, flipping halfway through.
4. In a baking dish, spread a layer of marinara sauce, followed by a layer of baked eggplant slices. Top with more marinara sauce and shredded mozzarella.
5. Repeat the layers and bake for an additional 15-20 minutes, until the cheese is melted and bubbly.
6. Garnish with fresh basil and serve hot.

Baked Lemon Herb Salmon

Ingredients

- 4 salmon fillets
- 2 tbsp olive oil
- 1 lemon, sliced
- 3 garlic cloves, minced
- 1 tbsp fresh parsley, chopped
- 1 tsp dried thyme
- Salt and pepper, to taste

Instructions

1. Preheat the oven to 375°F (190°C).
2. Place the salmon fillets on a baking sheet lined with parchment paper.
3. Drizzle with olive oil and season with salt, pepper, garlic, thyme, and parsley.
4. Top each fillet with a few slices of lemon.
5. Bake for 15-20 minutes, until the salmon flakes easily with a fork.
6. Serve with extra lemon wedges and garnish with fresh herbs.

Stuffed Acorn Squash with Quinoa

Ingredients

- 2 acorn squash, halved and seeded
- 1 tbsp olive oil
- 1 cup cooked quinoa
- 1/2 cup cranberries
- 1/4 cup chopped pecans
- 1/2 tsp cinnamon
- Salt and pepper, to taste
- 1 tbsp maple syrup (optional)

Instructions

1. Preheat the oven to 400°F (200°C).
2. Drizzle the squash halves with olive oil and season with salt and pepper.
3. Place the squash cut-side down on a baking sheet and roast for 25-30 minutes, until tender.
4. While the squash is baking, mix the quinoa, cranberries, pecans, cinnamon, and maple syrup in a bowl.
5. Once the squash is tender, remove it from the oven and stuff each half with the quinoa mixture.
6. Return to the oven for an additional 5-10 minutes, until heated through.
7. Serve as a hearty vegetarian dish.

Roasted Root Vegetables with Olive Oil

Ingredients

- 2 carrots, peeled and cut into chunks
- 2 parsnips, peeled and cut into chunks
- 1 sweet potato, peeled and cut into cubes
- 1 red onion, cut into wedges
- 2 tbsp olive oil
- 1 tsp dried thyme
- Salt and pepper, to taste

Instructions

1. Preheat the oven to 400°F (200°C).
2. Place the carrots, parsnips, sweet potato, and onion on a baking sheet.
3. Drizzle with olive oil, and sprinkle with thyme, salt, and pepper.
4. Toss to coat evenly.
5. Roast for 30-35 minutes, stirring once halfway through, until the vegetables are tender and lightly caramelized.
6. Serve as a flavorful side dish.

Chicken and Brown Rice Casserole

Ingredients

- 2 chicken breasts, cooked and shredded
- 1 cup cooked brown rice
- 1 cup broccoli florets, steamed
- 1 cup low-fat cream of mushroom soup
- 1/2 cup shredded cheese (optional)
- 1/4 tsp garlic powder
- Salt and pepper, to taste

Instructions

1. Preheat the oven to 375°F (190°C).
2. In a mixing bowl, combine the shredded chicken, cooked rice, steamed broccoli, and cream of mushroom soup.
3. Season with garlic powder, salt, and pepper.
4. Pour the mixture into a greased casserole dish and sprinkle with cheese if using.
5. Bake for 20-25 minutes, until the casserole is bubbly and the cheese is melted.
6. Serve hot as a comforting one-dish meal.

Black Bean and Sweet Potato Chili

Ingredients

- 2 medium sweet potatoes, peeled and cubed
- 2 cans (15 oz) black beans, drained and rinsed
- 1 can (14.5 oz) diced tomatoes
- 1 onion, diced
- 1 bell pepper, diced
- 2 garlic cloves, minced
- 2 tsp chili powder
- 1 tsp cumin
- Salt and pepper, to taste
- 1 tbsp olive oil
- Fresh cilantro, for garnish

Instructions

1. Heat olive oil in a large pot over medium heat.
2. Add the onion, bell pepper, and garlic, and cook for 5-7 minutes until softened.
3. Add the sweet potatoes, black beans, diced tomatoes, chili powder, cumin, salt, and pepper.
4. Stir to combine, and bring to a simmer.
5. Cover and cook for 20-25 minutes, until the sweet potatoes are tender.
6. Garnish with fresh cilantro and serve hot.

Zucchini Fritters with Greek Yogurt Dip

Ingredients for Fritters

- 2 medium zucchinis, grated
- 1/4 cup breadcrumbs
- 1 egg, beaten
- 2 tbsp grated Parmesan cheese
- 1 garlic clove, minced
- 1 tsp dried oregano
- Salt and pepper, to taste
- Olive oil, for frying

Ingredients for Greek Yogurt Dip

- 1/2 cup Greek yogurt
- 1 tbsp lemon juice
- 1 tbsp fresh dill, chopped
- Salt and pepper, to taste

Instructions

1. In a large bowl, mix the grated zucchini, breadcrumbs, egg, Parmesan cheese, garlic, oregano, salt, and pepper.
2. Heat olive oil in a skillet over medium heat.
3. Form the zucchini mixture into small patties and fry in batches for 3-4 minutes on each side, until golden brown and crispy.
4. In a small bowl, combine the Greek yogurt, lemon juice, dill, salt, and pepper.
5. Serve the fritters hot with the yogurt dip on the side.

Lentil Tacos with Guacamole

Ingredients for Lentil Filling

- 1 cup dried lentils, rinsed
- 2 cups vegetable broth
- 1 onion, diced
- 2 garlic cloves, minced
- 1 tsp chili powder
- 1 tsp cumin
- Salt and pepper, to taste
- 1 tbsp olive oil

Ingredients for Guacamole

- 2 ripe avocados, mashed
- 1/2 red onion, finely chopped
- 1 small tomato, diced
- 1 tbsp lime juice
- Salt and pepper, to taste

Instructions

1. In a pot, combine the lentils and vegetable broth. Bring to a boil, then reduce heat and simmer for 20-25 minutes until tender. Drain any excess liquid.
2. Heat olive oil in a skillet over medium heat. Add the onion and garlic and sauté for 5 minutes.
3. Add the cooked lentils, chili powder, cumin, salt, and pepper. Stir to combine and cook for an additional 5 minutes.
4. To make the guacamole, mash the avocados in a bowl and stir in the onion, tomato, lime juice, salt, and pepper.
5. Serve the lentil filling in soft tortillas and top with guacamole.

Grilled Portobello Mushrooms with Balsamic Glaze

Ingredients

- 4 large portobello mushrooms, stems removed
- 2 tbsp balsamic vinegar
- 1 tbsp olive oil
- 1 garlic clove, minced
- 1 tsp dried thyme
- Salt and pepper, to taste

Instructions

1. Preheat the grill to medium-high heat.
2. In a small bowl, whisk together the balsamic vinegar, olive oil, garlic, thyme, salt, and pepper.
3. Brush the mushrooms with the balsamic mixture on both sides.
4. Grill the mushrooms for 4-5 minutes per side, until tender and slightly charred.
5. Serve hot as a savory vegetarian main or side dish.

Broccoli and Cheddar Quiche

Ingredients

- 1 pre-made pie crust
- 1 cup broccoli florets, steamed
- 1 cup shredded cheddar cheese
- 4 large eggs
- 1 cup milk
- 1/2 tsp salt
- 1/4 tsp pepper
- 1/4 tsp nutmeg (optional)

Instructions

1. Preheat the oven to 375°F (190°C).
2. In a bowl, whisk together the eggs, milk, salt, pepper, and nutmeg.
3. Layer the steamed broccoli and cheddar cheese evenly in the pie crust.
4. Pour the egg mixture over the broccoli and cheese.
5. Bake for 35-40 minutes, or until the quiche is set and lightly browned on top.
6. Let it cool slightly before slicing and serving.

Spaghetti with Roasted Tomato Sauce

Ingredients

- 2 cups cherry tomatoes, halved
- 4 cloves garlic, peeled
- 1 tbsp olive oil
- Salt and pepper, to taste
- 1 tsp dried basil
- 1 tsp dried oregano
- 1 lb spaghetti
- Fresh basil leaves, for garnish
- Parmesan cheese, for serving (optional)

Instructions

1. Preheat the oven to 400°F (200°C).
2. Toss the cherry tomatoes and garlic with olive oil, salt, pepper, and dried herbs.
3. Roast on a baking sheet for 20-25 minutes, until tomatoes are soft and caramelized.
4. Meanwhile, cook the spaghetti according to package instructions.
5. Once the tomatoes are roasted, mash them lightly with a fork and toss with the cooked spaghetti.
6. Serve with fresh basil and grated Parmesan, if desired.

Grilled Shrimp with Cilantro-Lime Rice

Ingredients for Shrimp

- 1 lb shrimp, peeled and deveined
- 2 tbsp olive oil
- 1 tsp chili powder
- 1/2 tsp paprika
- Salt and pepper, to taste

Ingredients for Rice

- 1 cup long-grain rice
- 2 cups water
- 1 lime, zested and juiced
- 2 tbsp chopped fresh cilantro

Instructions

1. For the rice, bring 2 cups of water to a boil. Add rice, reduce heat to low, and cover. Cook for 18-20 minutes until rice is tender.
2. Fluff the rice with a fork and stir in lime zest, lime juice, and chopped cilantro.
3. For the shrimp, toss the shrimp in olive oil, chili powder, paprika, salt, and pepper.
4. Grill the shrimp for 2-3 minutes per side, until pink and cooked through.
5. Serve the grilled shrimp over the cilantro-lime rice.

Baked Turkey Breast with Rosemary

Ingredients

- 1 boneless turkey breast (about 3-4 lbs)
- 2 tbsp olive oil
- 2 cloves garlic, minced
- 2 tbsp fresh rosemary, chopped
- Salt and pepper, to taste
- 1/2 cup chicken broth

Instructions

1. Preheat the oven to 375°F (190°C).
2. Rub the turkey breast with olive oil, garlic, rosemary, salt, and pepper.
3. Place the turkey in a roasting pan and pour chicken broth around it.
4. Roast for 1.5-2 hours, or until the turkey reaches an internal temperature of 165°F (74°C).
5. Let the turkey rest for 10 minutes before slicing and serving.

Veggie-Packed Minestrone Soup

Ingredients

- 1 tbsp olive oil
- 1 onion, diced
- 2 carrots, peeled and diced
- 2 celery stalks, diced
- 2 garlic cloves, minced
- 1 zucchini, diced
- 1 cup green beans, chopped
- 1 can (14.5 oz) diced tomatoes
- 1 can (15 oz) cannellini beans, drained and rinsed
- 4 cups vegetable broth
- 1/2 cup small pasta (such as elbow macaroni or ditalini)
- Salt and pepper, to taste
- Fresh basil, for garnish

Instructions

1. Heat olive oil in a large pot over medium heat. Add the onion, carrots, and celery, and sauté for 5-7 minutes until softened.
2. Add the garlic, zucchini, green beans, diced tomatoes, cannellini beans, vegetable broth, salt, and pepper.
3. Bring to a boil, then reduce the heat and simmer for 20-25 minutes.
4. Stir in the pasta and cook for an additional 10 minutes until tender.
5. Serve with fresh basil on top.

Grilled Veggie and Hummus Wraps

Ingredients

- 1 zucchini, sliced
- 1 red bell pepper, sliced
- 1 yellow bell pepper, sliced
- 1 small red onion, sliced
- 1 tbsp olive oil
- Salt and pepper, to taste
- 1/2 cup hummus
- 4 whole wheat tortillas
- Fresh spinach or arugula

Instructions

1. Preheat the grill to medium heat.
2. Toss the sliced vegetables with olive oil, salt, and pepper. Grill the vegetables for 3-4 minutes per side, until tender and lightly charred.
3. Spread hummus on each tortilla.
4. Top with grilled veggies and fresh spinach or arugula.
5. Roll up the wraps and serve.

Roasted Butternut Squash with Garlic and Sage

Ingredients

- 1 medium butternut squash, peeled and cubed
- 2 tbsp olive oil
- 3 garlic cloves, minced
- 6 sage leaves, chopped
- Salt and pepper, to taste

Instructions

1. Preheat the oven to 400°F (200°C).
2. Toss the butternut squash cubes with olive oil, garlic, sage, salt, and pepper.
3. Spread the squash evenly on a baking sheet and roast for 25-30 minutes, until tender and lightly browned.
4. Serve as a savory side dish.

Black Bean and Quinoa Salad

Ingredients

- 1 cup cooked quinoa
- 1 can (15 oz) black beans, drained and rinsed
- 1 cup corn kernels (fresh, frozen, or canned)
- 1 red bell pepper, diced
- 1/4 cup fresh cilantro, chopped
- 1 lime, juiced
- 2 tbsp olive oil
- Salt and pepper, to taste

Instructions

1. In a large bowl, combine the quinoa, black beans, corn, red bell pepper, and cilantro.
2. Drizzle with lime juice and olive oil.
3. Toss everything together and season with salt and pepper.
4. Serve chilled or at room temperature.

Lemon Garlic Roasted Chicken

Ingredients

- 1 whole chicken (about 4 lbs)
- 2 tbsp olive oil
- 4 cloves garlic, minced
- 1 lemon, sliced
- 2 tbsp fresh rosemary, chopped
- 1 tbsp fresh thyme, chopped
- Salt and pepper, to taste

Instructions

1. Preheat the oven to 425°F (220°C).
2. Rub the chicken with olive oil, minced garlic, rosemary, thyme, salt, and pepper.
3. Stuff the chicken cavity with lemon slices.
4. Place the chicken on a roasting rack in a roasting pan.
5. Roast for 1.5-2 hours, or until the chicken reaches an internal temperature of 165°F (74°C).
6. Let the chicken rest for 10 minutes before carving and serving.

Baked Sweet Potato Fries

Ingredients

- 2 large sweet potatoes, peeled and cut into fries
- 2 tbsp olive oil
- 1/2 tsp paprika
- 1/2 tsp garlic powder
- Salt and pepper, to taste

Instructions

1. Preheat the oven to 425°F (220°C).
2. Toss the sweet potato fries with olive oil, paprika, garlic powder, salt, and pepper.
3. Arrange the fries in a single layer on a baking sheet.
4. Bake for 25-30 minutes, flipping halfway through, until crispy and golden.
5. Serve with your favorite dipping sauce.

Grilled Tofu Stir-Fry with Veggies

Ingredients

- 1 block firm tofu, pressed and cut into cubes
- 1 tbsp soy sauce
- 1 tbsp olive oil
- 1 bell pepper, sliced
- 1 zucchini, sliced
- 1 carrot, julienned
- 1 cup snap peas
- 2 tbsp sesame oil
- 1 tbsp soy sauce
- 1 tbsp rice vinegar
- 1 tsp grated ginger
- 1 tsp garlic, minced

Instructions

1. Preheat the grill or a grill pan over medium-high heat.
2. Toss tofu cubes with soy sauce and olive oil, then grill for 3-4 minutes per side until crispy.
3. In a large skillet, heat sesame oil over medium heat. Add the bell pepper, zucchini, carrot, and snap peas, and stir-fry for 5-7 minutes until tender.
4. Stir in the soy sauce, rice vinegar, ginger, and garlic.
5. Add the grilled tofu to the skillet and toss everything together.
6. Serve hot, garnished with sesame seeds or green onions.

Low-Sodium Beef Stew with Vegetables

Ingredients

- 1 lb lean beef stew meat, cubed
- 1 tbsp olive oil
- 1 onion, chopped
- 2 carrots, sliced
- 2 celery stalks, chopped
- 4 cloves garlic, minced
- 1 cup low-sodium beef broth
- 1 can (14.5 oz) diced tomatoes
- 2 cups water
- 1 tsp dried thyme
- 1 tsp dried rosemary
- Salt and pepper, to taste
- 2 potatoes, cubed
- 1 cup green beans, chopped

Instructions

1. Heat olive oil in a large pot over medium-high heat. Brown the beef stew meat on all sides, then remove and set aside.
2. In the same pot, sauté the onion, carrots, celery, and garlic for 5-7 minutes until softened.
3. Add the beef broth, diced tomatoes, water, thyme, rosemary, salt, and pepper.
4. Return the beef to the pot, bring to a boil, then reduce the heat and simmer for 1 hour.
5. Add the potatoes and green beans, and cook for an additional 30 minutes until tender.
6. Serve hot, garnished with fresh parsley if desired.

Vegan Lentil Loaf

Ingredients

- 1 cup dried lentils, cooked
- 1/2 cup oats
- 1/2 cup breadcrumbs
- 1/2 onion, finely chopped
- 2 cloves garlic, minced
- 1/2 cup tomato sauce
- 2 tbsp soy sauce
- 1 tbsp ground flaxseed (optional, for binding)
- 1 tsp dried thyme
- 1/2 tsp smoked paprika
- Salt and pepper, to taste
- 1/2 cup ketchup (for topping)

Instructions

1. Preheat the oven to 375°F (190°C).
2. In a large bowl, combine the cooked lentils, oats, breadcrumbs, onion, garlic, tomato sauce, soy sauce, flaxseed (if using), thyme, paprika, salt, and pepper.
3. Mash the mixture together until well combined.
4. Transfer the mixture into a greased loaf pan and press down firmly.
5. Spread the ketchup over the top of the loaf.
6. Bake for 40-45 minutes, until the loaf is firm and golden on top.
7. Let it cool slightly before slicing and serving.

Roasted Chickpeas for Snacking

Ingredients

- 1 can (15 oz) chickpeas, drained and rinsed
- 1 tbsp olive oil
- 1 tsp paprika
- 1/2 tsp garlic powder
- Salt and pepper, to taste

Instructions

1. Preheat the oven to 400°F (200°C).
2. Pat the chickpeas dry with a paper towel to remove excess moisture.
3. Toss the chickpeas with olive oil, paprika, garlic powder, salt, and pepper.
4. Spread the chickpeas in a single layer on a baking sheet.
5. Roast for 25-30 minutes, stirring halfway through, until crispy and golden.
6. Let cool and enjoy as a crunchy snack.

Baked Chicken Tenders with Almond Flour

Ingredients

- 1 lb chicken tenders
- 1 cup almond flour
- 1/2 tsp garlic powder
- 1/2 tsp paprika
- Salt and pepper, to taste
- 2 large eggs, beaten
- 2 tbsp olive oil

Instructions

1. Preheat the oven to 400°F (200°C) and line a baking sheet with parchment paper.
2. In a shallow bowl, combine the almond flour, garlic powder, paprika, salt, and pepper.
3. Dip each chicken tender into the beaten eggs, then coat with the almond flour mixture.
4. Arrange the coated chicken tenders on the baking sheet.
5. Drizzle with olive oil and bake for 20-25 minutes, flipping halfway through, until golden brown and cooked through.
6. Serve with your favorite dipping sauce.

Spaghetti Squash with Garlic and Olive Oil

Ingredients

- 1 medium spaghetti squash
- 2 tbsp olive oil
- 4 cloves garlic, minced
- Salt and pepper, to taste
- Fresh parsley, chopped (optional)

Instructions

1. Preheat the oven to 400°F (200°C).
2. Slice the spaghetti squash in half lengthwise and scoop out the seeds.
3. Drizzle with 1 tablespoon of olive oil and season with salt and pepper.
4. Place the squash halves cut-side down on a baking sheet and roast for 35-40 minutes until tender.
5. While the squash is roasting, heat the remaining olive oil in a skillet over medium heat and sauté the garlic for 1-2 minutes until fragrant.
6. Once the squash is done, use a fork to scrape out the spaghetti-like strands. Toss with the garlic and olive oil.
7. Garnish with fresh parsley and serve.

Avocado and Tomato Salad with Balsamic Dressing

Ingredients

- 2 ripe avocados, diced
- 2 cups cherry tomatoes, halved
- 1/4 red onion, thinly sliced
- 2 tbsp balsamic vinegar
- 1 tbsp olive oil
- Salt and pepper, to taste
- Fresh basil leaves, chopped (optional)

Instructions

1. In a large bowl, combine the diced avocado, cherry tomatoes, and red onion.
2. In a small bowl, whisk together the balsamic vinegar, olive oil, salt, and pepper.
3. Pour the dressing over the salad and gently toss to combine.
4. Garnish with fresh basil leaves, if desired, and serve immediately.

Baked Veggie Quesadillas

Ingredients

- 4 whole wheat tortillas
- 1 cup shredded cheese (cheddar, mozzarella, or a blend)
- 1 cup bell peppers, sliced
- 1/2 cup red onion, sliced
- 1/2 cup zucchini, thinly sliced
- 1/2 cup corn kernels
- 1 tbsp olive oil
- Salt and pepper, to taste

Instructions

1. Preheat the oven to 375°F (190°C) and line a baking sheet with parchment paper.
2. Heat olive oil in a skillet over medium heat and sauté the bell peppers, onion, zucchini, and corn for 5-7 minutes until softened. Season with salt and pepper.
3. Place two tortillas on the baking sheet and sprinkle each with cheese.
4. Spoon the sautéed veggies evenly over the cheese, then top with the remaining tortillas.
5. Bake for 10-12 minutes, flipping halfway through, until the tortillas are crispy and golden.
6. Slice and serve with salsa or guacamole.

Sweet Potato and Kale Salad

Ingredients

- 2 medium sweet potatoes, peeled and diced
- 1 tbsp olive oil
- 1/2 tsp cinnamon
- Salt and pepper, to taste
- 4 cups kale, chopped
- 1/4 cup olive oil
- 1 tbsp apple cider vinegar
- 1 tsp honey (optional)
- 1/4 cup pumpkin seeds

Instructions

1. Preheat the oven to 400°F (200°C).
2. Toss the diced sweet potatoes with olive oil, cinnamon, salt, and pepper.
3. Spread them in a single layer on a baking sheet and roast for 20-25 minutes until tender and slightly caramelized.
4. While the sweet potatoes are roasting, massage the chopped kale with 1/4 cup olive oil, apple cider vinegar, and honey (if using) until softened.
5. Once the sweet potatoes are done, allow them to cool slightly before adding them to the kale.
6. Toss the salad and sprinkle with pumpkin seeds before serving.